WHAT THE BIBLE SAYS

Mystery Babylon

What the Bible Says:

Mystery Babylon

Published by: Armor Books
P. O. Box 1050
Lawrenceville, GA 30045
Web Site: http://www.armorbooks.com
All rights reserved.

This is a derivative writing taken from the collective works of the late Finis Jennings Dake, and used by permission of the copyright holders. Unless otherwise noted, all Scripture quotations are from the Holy Bible, King James Version

Copyright © 2003 by Armor Books

First Printing 2003

Printed in the United States of America.

ISBN: 1-55829-079-6 (paperback)

01 02 03 04 05   87654321

CONTENTS

PREFACE

For many Christians, the Bible is a book of mystery, full of hidden meaning only to be understood by pastors and seminarians who have devoted lifetimes to uncovering the truths found within its pages. Latin was the language of the Bible for centuries, and many still approach the Scriptures as if they were written in a foreign tongue. A few stories are learned in Sunday School, a handful of popular verses memorized, but many Christians fear to turn the pages of their Bibles into unfamiliar territory.

But there is no reason to be afraid. The Bible is the easiest book in the world to understand. You don't need to be a pastor or have a seminary degree. God designed the Bible to be understood by everyone, and the truths He intended for us to learn are easily found within its pages.

The "*What the Bible Says*" booklets are designed to illustrate simple biblical truths on topics that many consider to be particularly difficult to grasp. This book strives to let the Bible speak for itself, and therefore, a comprehensive list of scripture references for each of the topics discussed will be presented. Although it's not necessary to look up each and every reference in order to understand what the Bible is saying on a particular topic, we'll focus on the primary references, and give you a thorough list of supporting scriptures for you to study on your own.

HOW TO UNDERSTAND THE BIBLE

Here's the most important rule to follow when studying the Bible: You must take the Bible literally wherever it is at all possible. Obviously, there are times when the language of the Bible cannot be taken literally, it is then we know it is to be understood figuratively. When this is the case, it is our job to find the literal truth conveyed by the figurative language, just as if it were expressed in literal language without the use of figures. For more on this topic, see Appendix I.

FIGURATIVE LANGUAGE OF THE BIBLE

The Bible contains some figurative language. A lot of confusion is caused when literal passages of Scripture are mistakenly understood figuratively, and the same holds true for Scripture that is interpreted as literal, when it is obviously figurative in nature. So what is figurative language in the Bible? How can we recognize it when we find it? Simply put, figurative language, or a "figure of speech" occurs when we use words in a different sense from that which is ordinarily given them. Figures of speech are used to give emphasis and to add attraction and variety to human expression. It is important to note that they are never used for the purpose of doing away with literal truth. Instead, figures of speech set forth literal truth in another form than that in which it could be literally expressed. What we're looking for is the literal truth found in the figurative language. Above all, we must not permit figures of speech to do away with the intended truth. If we fail to understand the literal truth expressed by the figure of speech, then it has failed in its purpose.

Now that we understand figures of speech, how can we tell whether a particular statement is intended to be understood literally or figuratively? It's easy! There's a fundamental rule to keep in mind when determining whether the language is literal or figurative: Every statement in the Bible is to be understood literally, when at all possible, and where it is clear that it is literal; otherwise, it is

Above all, we must not permit figures of speech to do away with the intended truth. If we fail to understand the literal truth expressed by the figure of speech, then it has failed in its purpose.

figurative. In other words, what cannot be literal must be figurative. The subject matter itself will always make this clear.

There are two kinds of figures of speech we find in the Bible: first, there are those involving only a word, as in Gal. 2:9 where Peter, James, and John are called "pillars" of the church; second, there are those involving a thought expressed in several words or sentences, such as the parable, allegory, symbol, type, riddle, fable, and enigma.

GOD'S PROMISES ARE ESPECIALLY SIMPLE

We've stated that many people think the Bible is hard to understand. In particular, this belief is held by many concerning the prophecies, the proverbs, and some figures of speech. However, these seemingly difficult parts of the Bible are no more difficult to understand and the sections of the Bible that deal with history, or those that many consider to be "simple." Prophecy is nothing more than history written beforehand and should be understood in this light. All riddles, allegories, types, symbols, and figures of speech are either explained in Scripture, or are clear in themselves as to their true meaning.

When it comes to the promises of God, there shouldn't be any misunderstanding about what they say or mean. Every promise of God is a simple statement of obligation to men that God will give them certain benefits when they meet certain conditions. All the promises of God are conditional, as can be seen in the Scriptures themselves. If you want to receive the promised benefits, you must accept the promise for what it says and meet the conditions required. You can then depend upon the fulfillment of God's promise *in this life*. Since God cannot lie, man is assured that what God has promised He is abundantly able to perform. None of God's promises need further interpretation. All that we must do is act upon what the Bible says and believe that God's promise will be fulfilled in our lives. Do not attach any other conditions to God's promises than what is plainly written. When the conditions are met the blessings will be realized. As the Apostle Paul writes in 2 Cor. 1:20, "For ALL the promises of God in Him are yea, and in Him Amen, unto the glory of God by us."

Chapter One

MYSTERY BABYLON

And upon her forehead was a name written, MYSTERY, BABYLON THE GREAT, THE MOTHER OF HARLOTS AND ABOMINATIONS OF THE EARTH (Rev. 17:5)

The seventeenth chapter of Revelation gives us a detailed account of Ecclesiastical Babylon, her character, power, wickedness, judgment and eventual destruction by the Antichrist and the ten kings. In this passage we also find an explanation of the beast and its seven heads and ten horns. But, it's "Mystery Babylon" that is our focus for this study and it is with the first verse of the chapter that we'll begin.

This chapter is a parenthetical pause between the preceeding chapter, where we see the destruction of Literal Babylon (Rev. 16:17-21), and the complete description of

11

that destruction in Rev. 18:1-24. Although Rev. 17 is out of order chronologically with the chapters immediately before and after, it is placed here for a purpose—to show the contrast between Mystical Babylon and Literal Babylon, rather than to show its sequence of fulfillment. This religion is destroyed by the Antichrist and the ten kings in the middle of the Week so that the Antichrist worship may be established (Rev. 17:16-17). Since the worship of the Beast is found during the last 3½ years of the Week, Mystery Babylon must be destroyed at that time (Rev. 13:1-18). Man destroys Mystical Babylon (Rev. 17:16-17), and God destroys Literal Babylon (Rev. 18:5-8, 20).

God will put the idea into the minds of the ten kings to give their kingdoms to the Beast for the purpose of destroying Mystical Babylon (17:14-17), while this is not true in the case of Literal Babylon. The Beast and the ten kings will rejoice over the destruction of Mystical Babylon (Rev. 17:16-17) and they will mourn over the destruction of Literal Babylon (Rev. 18:9-19). Thus it is clear that there are two different Babylons found in Rev. 16:17–18:24.

The Identity of Mystical Babylon

There are many marks of identification proving Mystery Babylon to be a great religious system, but these marks do not conclusively prove it to be Roman Catholicism, as many have taught down through the centuries. The commonly accepted theory is that Roman Catholicism is the mother of harlots and the harlots are the many branches of Christianity, all of whom will become linked together again in the last days to fulfill Rev. 17. These scholars believe that Romanism will control the ten kings of Revised Rome and will dominate the Beast for a short time during his rise over the ten kings and until the middle of the Week. Then, the Beast and the ten kings will destroy her so that the Beast may be worshipped the last 3½ years of this age, Rev. 17:9-17.

These same scholars point out that the "harlot" is not a political organization, but a religious one with political aspirations. Having a present program to rule the world, she has always satisfied herself with the power of dictation through kings rather than by the direct ruling of kingdoms.

Those who claim that the great harlot is the Roman Catholic Church give the following arguments to prove their claims:

I. The Harlot is Identified by Her History

The harlot is identified as Roman Catholicism by her history, from her inauguration some centuries after John until the present day. The history of Romanism is that of Christendom from its beginning, through the gathering of local churches into an organization, and culminating into the one great religious apostate system known today as the Roman Catholic Church.

During the first century the churches were

composed of small groups of believers in a heathen community. Most of them were poor, except for the local congregation at Rome, which included believers of the higher social rank. Everywhere Christians were distinguished from the heathen by their brotherly love, moral earnestness and purity, confident gladness in Christian teachings, hope of the Lord's coming, etc. They were hated for these differences and, from the time of Nero (54–68 A.D.), the Roman government was hostile to them and tried suppression. Their worship was informal and was generally held in private houses. In the public meetings the services were carried on by the people, who took part as the Spirit moved them. Prayers, testimonies, singing of psalms, reading of the Old Testament and the writings of the apostles were all a part of the worship. Sometimes there was such eagerness to take part that disorder resulted. They often had a love feast or a common meal, the symbol of brotherly love, from which the unbeliever was barred. They did not have creeds or formal statements of belief. The so–called

Apostle's Creed was not used before the second century. All Christians held that they belonged to the universal church, for all were one in Christ. There was no general organization having control of the scattered churches. The apostles exercised certain authority over them but it was not formal or official as in an organization. Each congregation managed its own affairs. The churches had elders and presbyters, sometimes called *bishops*, meaning "one who has oversight," whose duties were the pastoral care, discipline, and financial affairs. They also had deacons which performed subordinate services of the same kind.

During the second and third centuries prior to the reign of Constantine, Christianity spread in many places and among all classes and ranks, through the medium of traveling missionaries, apologists or literary defenders of the Christian religion, teachers, and Christians generally. The Christians were persecuted in the first three centuries by the Roman government, not only for their clean lives, which were a standing condemnation of the prevalent religious customs and moral conduct, but also because they would not honor the state religion by paying worship to the statutes of the emperors. The churches went through ten persecutions until the time of Constantine, who established religious liberty, chiefly for the benefit of Christians. He caused a radical change in Christianity, raising its position in the empire and changing the standard of admission to the churches until thousands of pagans were admitted with all their pagan ideas and superstitions. Through this supposed liberation of Christianity by the emperor, who entered actively into the affairs of the churches, endeavoring to settle doctrinal disputes, and exercising authority among Christians, certain errors crept into the churches.

Rise of the Roman Catholic Church

The churches by this time had become organized so that Constantine could deal with an organization. In the second century, a loose federation of churches sprang up, having one form of belief, expressed in confessions much like the Apostles Creed, and one form of local church government. These churches in this federation called themselves the Catholic Church—*Catholic* meaning "universal." There were many churches which differed from this Catholic Church in belief and government. The statement of faith became the test of membership. The test of man's Christianity became, not so much his loyalty to Christ as his agreement with the church as to doctrine.

Distinction between the clergy and laymen, unknown in the apostolic age, was marked. Bishops, presbyters, and deacons were separated from the members of the churches. As the sacrificial idea of the Lord's Supper grew, the clergy were more and more called "priests." The office of bishop was magnified and those in that office sometimes thought they had authority from God to correct error and to forgive sins. The idea that asceticism was the way to holiness grew and led them to believe that the clergy ought not to marry. Later came the idea that when several churches were established in one town they should be under a bishop, and naturally, the bishops of larger towns rose to importance over those of the smaller towns. They were called "Metropolitans" and each of them began to rule over several bishops and their districts or dioceses. By a further centralization, five bishops rose to a higher rank, that of patriarchs. These were the bishops of Rome, Constantinople, Alexandria, Jerusalem, and Antioch.

In the fifth century, Augustine taught his doctrine of the nature of the Catholic Church, which was generally accepted. He believed that the first bishops of the church were appointed by the apostles, that the apostles received from Christ the gifts of the Holy Spirit for the care of the Church, who, in turn gave them to their first successors, the first bishops; that the successors of the first bishops held the original faith and could give Christian teaching which brought salvation; that only in the Catholic Church, the church of these bishops in apostolic succession, was there salvation. Augustine was not the first to teach these ideas but he worked for their acceptance more than anyone before him.

There came another step in the centralization of the government of the Catholic Church. Among the five patriarchs, the two most prominent were those of Rome and Constantinople, the two principal cities of the world. Several causes concurred to raise the Roman bishop to the higher place, the greatest being the fact that he was bishop of the ancient capital of the world. For centuries Rome had ruled the world. The bishop of Rome naturally had an authority that none other had, or could have. Another cause was the custom which sprang up making the bishop a court of appeal in church disputes. This was brought about by the influence of the emperors of Rome who encouraged the centralization of the church in Rome. From the fifth century, the so–called Petrine claim was accepted, which made the bishop at Rome head of the Church by divine right, since he was supposedly the successor to Peter, the first universal head of the Church. The general acceptance of this made it as certain as if it were really true. Then the policy of the Roman bishops of holding all the authority that this claim bestowed upon them and claiming still more, and taking every opportunity to use this power to further the elevation of the Roman bishop over all others was carried on. Leo I, sometimes called the "first Pope" (444–461) asserted his universal authority in the strongest terms and claimed the right to give commands to bishops everywhere. His claims were denied by the bishop at Constantinople and were resisted somewhat in the West, but opposition helped to increase his power as the universal bishop. The word "pope" was used in the fourth and fifth centuries as the title of any bishop, but it gradually came to be reserved for the bishop at Rome.

The full title of "Roman Catholic Church" did not come into use until the power of the Roman bishops as the universal head of the church was fully recognized. Thus, out of the independent churches of the apostolic age, grew the Catholic Church, having its complete graded organization, its clergy possessing spiritual authority over the people together with a definite creed calling those who would not accept their rule "heretical." This Catholic Church later became the Roman Catholic Church, completely dominated by the bishop of Rome.

The centralization of the church continued toward Rome until about 600 A.D. Gregory I was crowned and recognized the first universal bishop and pope. The popes were for some time chosen by the emperors, but that order was changed when Hildebrand procured the establishment of the college of cardinals with power to elect the pope. The power of the emperor diminished so much as to be negligible from 1058–1061 A.D. Hildebrand also conceived the idea that the pope should be the supreme temporal ruler of the world as well as the absolute head of the church. The Roman church reached the height of its power during the jurisdiction of Innocent III, who made and set aside rulers and did according to his will in the affairs of all the kingdoms of western Europe.

During the thirteenth century the church became master of the Holy Roman Empire and ruled without a rival. In 1294 A.D., after the papacy had lost much influence, Boniface VIII came to the throne. He attempted to surpass Hildebrand and Innocent III in manifestation of his power, endeavoring to excommunicate Philip of France, who answered him by sending men-of-arms and taking him prisoner for three days. This act of flagrant rebellion and humiliation broke the temporal power of the papacy and the popes went into "Babylonish Captivity" for sixty–nine years at Avignon, which is just across the Rhone River from French territory. Then the pope went back to Rome and the French cardinals elected a pope who set up his court at Avignon and two popes occupied the papal chair for a period of thirty years, being in opposition to each other during that time. A meeting for reconciliation was held and a new pope was elected, but the other two indignantly refused to resign and so there were three popes for a short time. The general council called at Constance, five years

23

later, deposed two, caused the other to resign, with a closed breach resulting. Martin V was elected and acknowledged by the whole church in 1414 A.D.

The popes continued to wield an influence upon temporal rulers until the reformation gained such headway that the Emperor Charles V came to Germany to settle the religious dispute. He failed and despairing of a doctrine of love, at the Diet of Augsburg, 1530, the Roman Catholic majority decreed that the Protestant cause should be put down by war. The war started in 1546 and the emperor was victorious on all sides until Maurice drove him out of Germany. Then the emperor gave the German affairs of the empire into the hands of his brother Ferdinand, who made peace at Augsburg in 1555. The reformation spread to many lands until today practically all lands are blessed with freedom of worship.

The opening of the nineteenth century saw the papacy in great humiliation. In 1801 Napoleon, then ruler of France, concluded a concordat with Pope Pius VII, which was a treaty defining the relations of the Roman Catholic Church and the government in France. By this "the church was harnessed to the state" being made in part subject to the government, yet also supported by it. These terms involved a serious loss of authority for the pope, but he was helpless before the all–powerful Napoleon. When the pope, as sovereign of the papal states, disobeyed his wishes in a matter of European policy, Napoleon entered Rome with an army, annexed the papal states and made the pope a prisoner in 1809. After Napoleon's downfall (1814) Pope Pius VII returned to Rome and re-established the papal states.

The rulers then controlling Europe were favorable to the church, which seized upon this opportunity to acquire much power. The church set its face against all modern progress and attempted to develop its medieval elements. The order of the Jesuits, the soldiers of the papacy, strove to gain the absolute supremacy of the pope and was successful. Pope Pius IX (1846-1878) outlined the policy of the Roman Church which exists today, assuming with gross bigotry, that limitless authority was his by divine right. He thus took upon himself the power and right to define doctrine, which, in the past had been exercised only by the general councils. The Council of Trent (1545) determined the complete statement of doctrine for the church. The Vatican Council was the next held (1870), adding more decrees and giving the pope unlimited and immediate authority in every part of the activities of the church and making him infallible in defining the doctrines and morals of the church.

In 1848, a movement began to free Italy from the papal supremacy and bring her under one standard. By 1860 both the northern and southern parts of Italy came under the rule of an Italian king, Victor Immanuel, of Piedmont. The Italians recognized that there could be no united Italy as long as the pope held full sway over the Papal States, stretching from sea to sea and with a population of 3 million. In 1870 the king added Rome and the Papal States to his domain, thus uniting the whole of Italy.

The pope was no longer the temporal ruler of Rome. Since then, it became the policy of the popes to remain voluntary prisoners in the Vatican and never walk the streets of Rome, for to do so, it was said, would be recognizing the claims of the government that ruled. Much was said and done concerning the restoration of the Papal States and finally on February 11, 1929, the Lateran Treaties were signed, the ceremony taking place at the Vatican Palace, which ended the long conflict between Italy and the Holy See and freed the popes from voluntary imprisonment.

One treaty, solving and eliminating the "Roman Question," which had existed since the loss of temporal power in 1870, and a second, a concordat designed to regulate the relations of the church and state in Italy, were signed. The canon law which is the subject of three of the four parts of the concordat was completed in 1917. It contains 2,417 canons,

27

or rules regulating faith, morals, conduct, and discipline of church members, which have been gradually added by the church throughout the centuries. These treaties were ratified May 14 and 25 and became effective June 7, 1929.

The pope is again temporal ruler and sovereign over a territory the size of a town of 20,000 people, known as the Vatican State or State of Vatican City. It now has power to coin money, issue bank notes, postage stamps and do as any other sovereign state. The pope has his own railway station, wireless station, aviation field, army and navy, etc. He is to receive indemnity from the Italian government of $87.5 million. This is a great boon to Romanism, for she now has a "free" pope to enter personally into world affairs. The Holy See maintains diplomatic relations with many nations.

Chapter Two

THE ANCIENT BABYLONIAN CULT

If this passage is indeed descriptive of the Roman Catholic Church, then what is the historic relation of Babylon to the city of Rome and the Roman Church, and why should Romanism be called Babylon in mystery? That the cities of Rome and Babylon were related seems to have been well known in earlier days. It is a simple matter to trace in the archives of history the relation of Babylon to Rome and to the Roman Church. Let us first look at the history of ancient Babylon.

This city was built by Nimrod, the mighty hunter (Gen. 10:8-10). It was the seat of the first great apostasy against God after the flood. Here the Babylonian Cult was invented by Nimrod and his queen, Semiramis. It was a system claiming the highest wisdom and ability to reveal the most divine secrets. This cult was characterized by the word "MYSTERY" because of its system of mysteries. Besides confessing to the priests at admission, one was compelled to drink of "mysterious beverages," which, says Salverte (*Des Sciences Occultes*, Page 259) was indispensable on the part of those who sought initiation into these mysteries." The "mysterious beverages" were composed of wine, honey, water, and flour. They were always of an intoxicating nature, and until the aspirants had come under the influence of it and had their understanding dimmed they were not prepared for what they were to see and hear. The method was to introduce privately, little by little, information under seal of secrecy and sanction of oath that would be impossible to reveal otherwise. Once admitted, men were no longer Babylonians, Assyrians, or Egyptians, but were members of a mystical brotherhood, over whom was placed a High Priest whose word was final in the lives of the brotherhood, regardless of the country in which they lived.

The ostensible objects of worship were the

Supreme Father, the Incarnate Female, or Queen of Heaven, and her Son. The last two were really the only objects of worship, as the Supreme Father was said not to interfere with mortal affairs (*Nimrod III*, Page 239). This system is believed to have come from fallen angels and demons. The object of the cult was to rule the world by these dogmas.

How the Ancient Babylonian Cult Spread

In the days of Nimrod this cult secured a deep hold on the whole human race for it was of one language and all were one people. Nimrod gained the title "mighty Hunter" because of his success in building cities with walls to free men from the ravages of wild beasts which were multiplying against men. He was called "the Apostate" because he sought to free men from the concept of God and His wrath. As a great deliverer and protector of the people, and as the head of the godless civilization at that time, he would naturally have great influence upon the people. He led them astray to such an extent that they gloried in the fact that they were free from the faith of their fathers.

Historical tradition from the earliest time bears witness to this great apostasy, which finally reached such proportions that the people defied God to send another flood to destroy them and they built a tower to escape it. The result was that God confused their language and scattered them throughout the earth. This Babylonian system was the one which the devil had planned to counteract the truth of God. From Babylon it spread to the ends of the earth and we have record that Abraham was chosen of God from all these idolatrous nations to represent the true God. Through him God planned to bring man back to Himself. This explains how the different nations of the world have traditions and religions somewhat similar, with changes suitable to the individual nation.

After the nations were scattered abroad, Babylon continued to be the "seat of Satan" until it was taken by Xerxes in 487 B.C. The

Babylonian priesthood was then forced to leave Babylon, so it moved to Pergamos, which was the headquarters for some time. When Attalus, the Pontiff (High Priest) and king of Pergamos, died in 133 B.C. he bequeathed the headship of the Babylonian priesthood to Rome. When the Etruscans came to Italy from Lydia (the region of Pergamos) they brought with them the Babylonian religion and rites. They set up a Pontiff who was the head of the priesthood and who had the power of life and death over them. Later, the Romans accepted this Pontiff as their civil ruler. Julius Caesar was made the Supreme Pontiff of the Etruscan Order in 74 B.C. In 63 B.C. he was made Supreme Pontiff of the Babylonian Order, thereby becoming heir to the rights and titles of Attalus, who had made Rome his heir by will.

Thus, the first Roman emperor became the head of the Babylonian priesthood and Rome became the successor of Babylon with Pergamos as the seat of this cult. Henceforth, Rome's religion has been that of Babylon. In the year 218 A.D. the Roman army in Syria, having rebelled against Macrinus, elected Elagabalus emperor. This man was High Priest of the Egyptian branch of Babylonianism. He was shortly afterward chosen Supreme Pontiff by the Romans, and thus the two Western branches of the Babylonian apostasy centered in the Roman Emperors who continued to hold this office until 376 A.D. At that time, however, the Emperor Gratian, for Christian reasons refused it, because he saw that by nature Babylonianism was idolatrous. Thus, religious matters became disorganized until it became necessary to elect someone to fill the office.

The Babylonian Religion and Roman Christendom United

Damasus, bishop of the Christian Church at Rome, was then elected to the office of supreme pontiff. He had been bishop for twelve years, having been made such in 366 A.D. through the influence of the monks of Mount Carmel, a college of the Babylonian religion originally founded by the priests of Jezebel and continued to this day in connection with Rome. So, in 378 A.D., the Babylonian system of religion became part of Christendom, for the bishop of Rome, who later became the supreme head of the organized church, was already Supreme Pontiff of the Babylonian Order. Many of the teachings of pagan Babylon and Rome were gradually interspersed into the Christian religious organization. Soon after Damasus was made Supreme Pontiff, the rites of Babylon began to come to the front. The worship of the Roman Church became Babylonish, and under him the heathen temples were restored and beautified and the rituals established. Thus, the corrupt religious system under the figure of a woman with a golden cup in her hand, making all nations drunk with her fornication, is called by God "MYSTERY, BABYLON THE GREAT."

Chapter Three

INTERESTING, BUT TRUE?

To say the least, the statements in the previous chapter are enlightening as to the history of the Roman Catholic Church, but they do not really prove that the great harlot is a symbol of Roman Catholicism. They leave too many questions unanswered. For example, why would the city of Rome be called Babylon when there is no connection between them? They are over 2,000 miles apart! Furthermore, whereas Rome is not once mentioned in prophecy, Babylon is mentioned scores of times—six times in Revelation alone. Apart from prophecy, Rome is mentioned only nine times, as compared to the 294 times Babylon is named throughout Scripture. And, the Roman Catholic Church is not mentioned once in the entire Bible, so why bring her into the picture at all?

The often repeated idea that Rome is a city on seven hills, which can be what Christ meant when He mentioned the seven heads on the beast as being seven mountains, does not hold up in the light of all that is said in the passage (Rev. 17:9-12) on the subject.

This could not be the intended thought, for the explanation makes it clear that five of these mountains had been in existence before John's time, only one was in existence when he saw the Revelation, and the seventh was yet to come. Then, there was to be an eighth—and this would completely do away with Rome and her so-called seven hills, as a fulfillment of the passage.

Regarding any points of similarity between the religion of Rome and that of Babylon, this would not prove them to be one and the same city any more than points of similarity between two men would prove them to be one and the same person. With two cities to consider and their two religions with some points of similarity, which one could we logically say was referred to as Mystery Babylon in Revelation 17? The one whose actual name is called in Revelation 17—or another?

Babylon, being a city, as it is stated, and her future religion must be the reference of Scripture, instead of Rome and her religion.

How could the so–called mysteries of the Roman Church, some of which we've mentioned, cause Rome to be Babylon? Actually, they are not "mysteries" at all but rather practices that have little or no basis in Scripture. Any number of practices adopted from Babylon by Rome could not make Rome to become Babylon, herself. And the same is true regarding the splitting up of Christians into many branches, as well as the present trend toward church unions—these do not prove Romanism to be the mother of harlots of Revelation 17.

How could the terms "the great harlot" and "the woman" prove Babylon to be Rome? The fact is, these terms are used in Scripture in connection with Israel, Babylon, and various pagan nations with whom Israel committed fornication long before there were Christians (Isa. 13:8; 54:6; Jer. 3:9; 4: 31; 6:2, 24; 13:27; 22:23; Lam. 1:17; Ezek.

16:17-36; 20:30; 23:3-44; 43:7-9; Hos. 4: 10-12; Zech. 5:5-11); but they do not prove the identity of any one more than another. Neither can these terms identify Babylon as Rome or Roman Christendom, for not once are they used of professing Christians in any sense or degree. Persons professing to be Christians are never called Babylon, Rome, a harlot, a woman, or anything else of the feminine gender, as a group in particular. The true Church, being the body of Christ who was a man, is therefore called a "man" in Scripture instead of a woman, as we see in Eph. 2:14-15; 4:13.

Truly the religion of witchcraft, demon worship, and demon manifestations, as mentioned in Rev. 9:20-21; 13:2, 12-18; 16: 13-16; 18:2; 19:2; Dan. 11:37-38; Mt. 24:24; 2 Thess. 2:8-12 best describe the religion of Babylon in the days after Antichrist. Such demon religion headed by Satan will be given to Antichrist and he will become the object of worship in the last 3½ years of this age, 2 Thess. 2:3-4, 8-12; Rev. 13; 17:12-18.

None can deny that the great harlot is a religious system with headquarters in a well-known city. In this all scholars agree. And so, the only points we could differ on are: which city—Rome or Babylon? and which religion—Christianity or ancient magism, spiritism, witchcraft, sorcery, idolatry, and paganism?

It cannot be denied that Roman Catholicism is basically a Christian religion with a firm faith in God, Christ, the Holy Spirit, the virgin birth, the death, burial, resurrection, and ascension of Jesus Christ to sit on the right hand of God, the blood atonement for sins, the forgiveness of sins by God through Jesus Christ, and other basic Christian doctrines and biblical facts. Therefore, Romanism as now constituted, even though it has some ancient Babylonian rituals and rites intermingled throughout, could not be Mystery Babylon of Revelation 17. To become the great harlot or Mystery Babylon and the kind of religion prevailing after the rapture of the Church, she would need to give up all of her true Christian truths and rites—and regarding this we have no proof that it will happen.

The religion of Mystery Babylon will be anti–God; and this cannot be said of Roman Catholicism. It must be remembered that the "things" of Rev. 4–22 "must be hereafter,"—after the churches—therefore, we have to understand Revelation 17 as referring to the religion of Babylon in the future, after the rapture of the Church. What then, could this religion possibly be?

The word "harlots" could very easily be understood as referring to the many branches of ancient demonism that were practiced among many nations, beginning with Babylon. The word "abominations" is used many times in Scripture, and long before the times of Christianity, of idolatry and harlot-doms associated with demon worship and the sorceries and witchcraft of all kinds that were practiced by many pagan nations, Dt. 18:9-12; 29:17-18; 32:16-17; 1 Ki. 14:24; 2 Ki. 16:3-4; 17:1-25; 21:2-11; Ezek. 16:22-58; etc.

Thirteen Proofs that the Harlot is a Religious Sysem:

1. "Playing the Harlot" in symbolic language always refers to religious fornication and idolatry (Rev. 17:1-4; Isa. 23:17; 53:3-7; Jer. 3:2-9; Ezek. 16:1-63; 20:30-32; 23:7-49; Hos. 4:12-19; Nah. 3:4). Literal fornication must also be understood in some of these.

2. Her causing the many nations to commit fornication with her, proves that idolatrous religious practices are being referred to, as in passages above.

3. She is not a political power for she is not classed as one with "the kings of the earth." She only causes the kings and inhabitants of the earth to be drunk with the wine of her fornication (Rev. 17:2, 4). Since fornication here refers to religious harlotry then her influence over the nations is through religion.

4. The beast which the woman rides is the 8th kingdom, made up of the many waters or peoples inside the old Roman

Empire territory (Rev. 17:1, 3, 11, 15). Since the beast itself is the kingdom, the woman must be religion dominating the kingdom until, in the end, she is finally destroyed by it (Rev. 17:12-17).

5. The attire of the great harlot identifies her as a religious system or as a harlot committing spiritual fornication, duping political powers by her harlotries and idolatries (Rev. 17:4). The purple, scarlet, precious stones, pearls, and golden vessels indicate the wealth of the system. Cp. Ezek. 23:40-41.

6. The golden cup in her hand, full of her uncleanness, spiritual fornication, and abominations by which she dupes political powers proves her to be a religious power. Cp. Ezek. 23:29-31.

7. Her name "Mystery Babylon" indicates she is not Literal Babylon. The word "mystery" identifies her with the religious rites and mysteries of ancient Babylon.

8. The name "Mother of Harlots" iden-

43

tifies the harlot as a religious system (Rev. 17:5). The harlots refer to many branches which have sprung from her and have become as much apostate as the great harlot herself. She is a symbol of apostate religions being linked together after the rapture of the Church to dominate the ten kings of the Revised Roman Empire until Antichrist comes to full power over the ten kingdoms by the middle of Daniel's Seventieth Week (Rev. 17:1, 3, 9-17).

9.   The name "Mother of Abominations of the Earth" identifies her to be a religious system, fostering and tolerating all the abominations that go with idolatry and spiritual fornication. The word "abominations" is used many times of idolatry and harlotries associated with pagan worship (Dt. 18:9-12; 29:17-18; 32:16-17; 1 Ki. 14:24; 2 Ki. 16:3-4; 21: 2-11; Ezek. 16:22-58; etc.). The great harlot of the future tribulations will be the mother of abominations in God's sight because she will exceed all others in wickedness.

10. Her drunkenness—being drunken

with blood of the martyrs of Jesus—proves beyond doubt that she is a religious institution. Only religion has killed the martyrs of Jesus in all ages. Governments have carried out the dictates of leaders in religion, doing the actual killing of saints because of religion. Although this prophecy speaks of the future drunkenness of Mystical Babylon after the rapture of the Church, who among us does not know of the martyrdom of 200,000,000 people in the past because they would not conform to organized religion?

Five Classes that have Martyred Saints:

(1) Jews (Acts 7:51-60; 8:1; 9:1). Their religious prejudice caused many to be put to death.
(2) Pagans of the old Roman Empire. History records the martyrdoms of many Christians by pagan emperors because of religious differences.
(3) Mohammedans slew Christians in all their conquests.

(4) Greek Catholics have also persecuted and martyred Christians.

(5) Roman Catholics have been guilty of martyrdoms in many centuries and many lands.

Martyrdom of saints will again be revived in the old Roman Empire territory between the rapture and the Second Advent. In the first 3½ years of Daniel's 70th Week, the great harlot will murder the saints of Jesus (Rev. 17:6). In the middle of the Week when Antichrist comes to power over the ten kingdoms the great harlot will be destroyed and martyrdom of Christians will be carried on by the Beast and the ten kings until the Second Advent (Rev. 13:1-18; 14:9-11; 17:9-17; 19:11–20:6).

11. The hatred and destruction of the great harlot by ten kings inside the Roman Empire territory prove her to be a religious system dominating them until they tire of her and give their power to the Antichrist. They then turn on the great harlot and destroy her so that the Antichrist might

establish the beast worship the last 3½ years (Rev. 17:12-17).

12.   The woman sits on the Beast itself, not on the heads and horns in succession (Rev. 17:1, 3, 7, 15). The seven heads and ten horns on the beast are a part of him and this is the only sense in which she rides the heads (Rev. 17:9). Since the beast is the eighth world empire (Rev. 17:11), it is clear that she is something separate from the empire, and only rides or dominates the peoples of that empire. What could she be other than religion?

13.   The angelic explanation of the great harlot proves her to be a religious system reigning over kings spiritually. The Greek reads, "And the woman whom thou sayest is the city the great, which has a kingdom over the kings of the earth" (Rev. 17:18). She has a kingdom within the kingdoms and over them. She is to be a religious system inside the old Roman Empire territory; one that has headquarters in a great city; and one that has a religious kingdom or reign over the kings of the earth.

We must recognize in the symbol two
things: a great religious system and a great
city where she has headquarters. The great
harlot will hold power over her loyal sub-
jects, not through superior military forces,
but by the deceptions of her spiritual harlotry
and abominations. That Babylon will be
the headquarters of this religious system is
proven by the following facts:

18 Reasons Babylon the City:

1. Literal Babylon is definitely the subject
   of Rev. 16:17-21 and 18:1-24.
2. Mystical Babylon is another subject
   inserted between these two passages,
   a parenthetical one to explain the religious aspect of Babylon.
3. The fact that the great harlot is called
   Mystery Babylon proves a connection
   with Literal Babylon (Rev. 17:5).
4. Literal Babylon is the site of the first
   great rebellion against God after the
   flood of Noah (Gen. 11) and it will be
   the site of the last great rebellion (Rev.

14:8; 16:17-21; 18:1-24).

5. Literal Babylon is always associated with demon religions and idolatry in Scripture (Isa. 21:9; 47:9-10; Rev. 18: 2-3, 23).

6. Many prophecies concerning Literal Babylon in both testaments are yet unfilled (Isa. 13:1-22; 14:1-27; 43:14; 47:1-15; 48:20; Jer. 50–51; Zech. 5:5-11; Rev. 14:8; 16:17-21; 18:1-24). On the other hand, the city of Rome is not once mentioned in any prophecy, fulfilled or unfulfilled.

7. Of all the empires taking part in the times of the Gentiles—Egypt, Assyria, Babylon, Medo-Persia, Greece, Rome, Revised Rome and Revived Greece, the capital city of only one (Babylon) is mentioned in prophecy with a latter day fulfillment. Memphis, Ninevah, Shushan, Rome, etc. are completely ignored in prophecy, while the capital city, Babylon, is mentioned repeatedly (See scriptures under point 6 above).

8. Never has it been necessary to re-

identify any city named in prophecy. Predictions in Scripture about Sodom, Gomorrah, Ninevah, Tyre, Sidon and others have been fulfilled regarding the cities known by the names referred to in the various passages. Why should Babylon be an exception? The word "mystery" simply defines the religious aspect of the literal city—Babylon.

9. Literal Babylon is the only city in Scripture called the "lady of kingdoms" (Isa. 47:5, 7).

10. Babylon is the only city of the last days that will be the headquarters for every demon and unclean spirit (Rev. 18:2). If this be true, then Rome or no other city will be the center of false religions fulfilling prophecy.

11. Babylon is the only city named making all nations drunk with the wine of her fornication (Rev.18:3). The great harlot unnamed is the only other Babylon causing nations to be drunk with the wine of her fornication, so the references must be to the same city—Mystery

Babylon being the religious aspect of Literal Babylon (Rev. 17:2).

12. Babylon is the only city in the last days to be the center of sorceries, enchantments, etc. (Rev. 18:23; Isa. 47:9-10, 12-13). Rome could not take Babylon's place in this.

13. Babylon is the only named city singled out as the object of God's wrath and plagues (Rev. 16:19; 18:4, 6). If Rome was to be the great city fulfilling such prophecy it surely would have been mentioned instead of Babylon, for Rome was as well known as Babylon at the time John wrote the Revelation. The very absence of the name "Rome" is no mere accident. God never leaves us in doubt as to the true meaning of His revelation of events to come.

14. Babylon is the only city God commands His people to come out of, in the last days (Rev. 18:4; Jer. 50:4-9; 51:4-8, 45). The application of this to Rome is out of harmony with Scripture.

15. Heaven is commanded to rejoice over

the destruction of Literal Babylon because God has taken vengeance on her (Rev. 18:20). This is the same as judging the great harlot of Revelation 17, proving that the great harlot or Mystical Babylon is the same as Literal Babylon as far as a place or a city is concerned (Rev. 19:2). The only difference is that the great harlot is the religious aspect of the city of Babylon.

16. Babylon is the only city named which is to be judged in the last days for martyrdoms (Rev. 18:24). Since both Mystery and Literal Babylons martyr the saints there must be some relationship. If two different cities as far from each other as Rome and Babylon were to be guilty of the same things after the rapture, then two places would be referred to and not one only as in Revelation 18:24.

17. The 16 points of contrast, 7 points of similarity, and 31 facts about Babylon in Rev. 16–18 are in harmony with the idea that the one Babylon, a literal city, is the headquarters of the other, Mystery

Babylon, a religious system.

18. Antichrist will be king of Syria with Babylon as his capital (Isa. 14:4). This will fulfill Dan. 8:8-9, 20-25; 11:35-45. The great harlot will ride the Beast (Antichrist's kingdom) in his rise to power over the ten kingdoms (Rev. 17: 3, 7). It should be recognized then, that she symbolizes a religion in his capital even before he gets power over the ten kingdoms of Revised Rome (Rev. 17: 12-17).

What religion is symbolized by the great harlot with headquarters at Babylon? Could Apostate Christendom have headquarters in Babylon? That is possible, but not probable, due to the fact that the religion predicted in Revelation 17 is anti-Christian. Could it be Islam, the religion of the eastern part of the Roman Empire territory? It could be, since Islam has as great a stronghold as Catholicism in the area. Muslims control the northern part of Africa, including Egypt, all of Arabia, Trans-Jordan, Syria, Iraq, Iran,

Turkey and other parts of the old Roman Empire territory. Catholicism is the prevailing religion in Albania, Bulgaria, Romania, Yugoslavia, Hungary, Austria, Italy, Spain, Portugal, France, and some other parts of the old Roman Empire territory. Between the two religions most of the old Roman Empire territory is covered religiously, but this does not prove anything regarding Mystery Babylon of Revelation 17.

The religion of Babylon could be a new religion entirely, or a revival of ancient sorcery, witchcraft, enchantments, and astrology which characterized the ancient city. It is clear that such will be the prevailing religion of the whole Roman Empire territory in the last days, as in point 12, above.

Jesus predicted many false prophets who would show great signs and wonders to deceive men just prior to His coming to earth again (Mt. 24:24). Paul predicted the coming of Antichrist with all power, signs, and lying wonders by the power of Satan (2 Th. 2:8-12; Rev. 13:1-18; 19:20). All nations will be deceived by the sorceries and manifestations of demon powers concentrated in future Literal Babylon (Rev. 9:20; 14:8; 16:13-16, 19; 18:23; Isa. 47:9-10, 12-13).

If the Antichrist can start a religion and martyr millions during the last 3½ years of this age (Rev. 7:9-17; 13:1-18; 14:9-11; 16: 2, 6; 16:13-16; 19:20; 20:4-6), then it stands to reason that Mystery Babylon, as a revival of ancient magism backed by a concentration of demonic powers dominating the nations of the old Roman Empire territory from Babylon, could martyr many saints of Jesus during the first 3½ years of Daniel's 70th week and until the Antichrist comes to full power over the ten kingdoms of Revised Rome (Rev. 17:1-2, 5-6, 12-17).

Both Catholicism and Islam would have to change completely to fulfill prophecies of these events.

One thing seems certain—Mystery and Literal Babylons are two aspects of the same city and the power that will fulfill prophecy in the last days after the rapture of the

Church. Mystery Babylon is a religious system with headquarters in Literal Babylon and will fulfill Revelation 17 until the Antichrist comes to full power over the ten kingdoms of Revised Rome in the middle of Daniel's Seventieth Week (Rev. 17:12-17). Then the Antichrist, who will be king of Babylon (Isa. 14:4) and the Assyrian (Isa. 10:20-27; 30: 18-33; 31:43; Mic. 5:3-15), will destroy this religious system and start his own worship the last 3½ years of this age (Rev. 13:1-18; 14:8-11; 15:2-4; 16:2, 6; 17:12-17; 20:4-6).

One thing must be kept in mind, all of these events will take place after the rapture of the Church, so Mystery Babylon need not be some religion now prominent inside the Roman Empire territory any more than the religion the Antichrist will start must be some prominent religion now in existence. Religions can begin in one day and so it will be easy for two religions (the Antichrist's and Babylon's) both to start and martyr millions between the rapture and the Second Coming of Jesus Christ.

Chapter Four

THE DESTRUCTION OF LITERAL BABYLON

The word "Babylon" is used 283 times in Scripture and only once in a symbolic sense (Rev. 17:5). Many do not believe in a future Literal Babylon and argue that it is in ruins today and will be forever, and that the Babylon of Revelation 18 is the same as the one in chapter 17. This line of argument does not prove that there will not be a Literal Babylon that will be destroyed as in Revelation 16:17-21; 18:1-24, nor does it prove that it is the same as chapter 17. There is to be a destruction of a literal city called Babylon under the seventh vial (Rev. 16:19), for no earthquake could destroy a religious system. All the other cities destroyed by the same earthquake are literal cities, so why shouldn't Babylon be as well? That there will be a literal city in the land of Shinar is very clear from the following scriptures:

Scriptural Proofs that Babylon Will Be Rebuilt Again

A. Babylon will be overthrown as God overthrew Sodom and Gomorrah (Isa. 13:19; Jer. 50:40). This prophecy has never been fulfilled by judgment from God in "one hour" (Rev. 18).

B. Babylon will never be inhabited after its final overthrow (Isa. 13:20; Jer. 50:39, 40; 51:29, 37, 43).

C. The final overthrow must be followed immediately by blessings on Israel (Isa. 13:6-17; 14:1-7; Jer. 50:4-7, 17-20, 33-35; Rev. 18–20).

D. The stones of ancient Babylon were not to be used for building purposes again (Jer. 51:26). Stones from the present ruins are being used again.

E. Babylon must be in existence in the future "day of the Lord" (Isa. 13:6-13; Rev. 16:17-21; 18:1-24; 19:1-3).

F. Babylon must be destroyed under the seventh vial and at the Second Advent of Christ or in "the day of the Lord" by a supernatural destruction (Isa. 13:6-13; Jer. 50:20, 40; 51:8; Rev. 16:17-21; 18: 8, 10, 17, 19, 21).

G. Babylon is to be destroyed at the end of the Great Tribulation when the planets are affected (Isa. 13:9-13; Matt. 24:29-31; Rev. 16:17-21).

H. Babylon is to be totally desolate and all sinners in it destroyed (Isa. 13:9, 19-22; Jer. 50:3, 23, 39, 40; 51:26, 29, 37, 43; Rev. 18:19, 21-24; 19:3). People now visit the ruins of ancient Babylon.

I. Babylon is to be destroyed at the time the world is punished for its sins at the Second Advent (Isa. 13:11; Rev. 18:1-24).

J. Babylon is to be destroyed when Christ comes with the armies of Heaven to fight at Armageddon (Isa. 13:1-5, 11-13; 14:5, 25-27; Rev. 16:17-21; 18:8; 19:1-3, 11-21).

K. The site of Babylon is to be one of the openings of Hell on earth where men will see the wicked in an everlasting burning Hell. Thus Babylon, the site of the first and last great apostasy against God, will be an everlasting monument of God's wrath, as will also all rebels of all ages who go to Hell (Isa. 14:9-17; 66:22-24; Rev. 19:3).

L. Babylon is to be destroyed in the day of Israel's final restoration and blessing at the Second Advent (Isa. 13:12; 14:1-8; Jer. 50:4-7, 19; 51:50, 51; Rev. 11:25-29).

M. Israel is to rule over her oppressors in the day of Babylon's final destruction (Isa. 14:1-4; Rev. 16:17-21; 18:1-24; Zech. 14).

N. The generation of Israel who enter the Millennium will sing a triumphant song over the Antichrist, the future king of Babylon, who will have persecuted them (Isa. 14:3-27).

O. Babylon is to be "suddenly" and in "one hour" destroyed (Isa 13:19; Jer. 50:40; 51:8; Rev. 18:8, 10, 17, 19). This has never been fulfilled for ancient Babylon fell into ruins gradually.

P. Babylon is to be a world commercial

center after the rapture of the Church. Revelation 4–22 will be fulfilled after the churches. Zechariah 5:5-11 predicts the rebuilding of such a center of commerce in the land of Shinar. There are 28 articles of commerce mentioned in Revelation 18, proving it to be a literal city.

Q. Babylon must again be a world political center (Rev. 18:3, 9, 10).

R. Babylon must again be a world religious center (Rev. 18:2-10).

S. Babylon's latter-day sorceries will deceive the world (Rev. 18:23; 2 Thess. 2:9-15).

T. Orders for the martyrdom of saints during the Great Tribulation will be decreed from this city (Rev. 18:24).

U. Babylon must be burned with fire (Rev. 18:8-10, 18; 19:3).

V. Babylon must be destroyed by an earthquake (Rev. 16:17-21).

W. Babylon must be thrown down with violence (Rev. 18:21).

X. Babylon must never be found after her destruction (Rev. 18:21).

Y. Babylon must sink into the earth (Jer. 51:62-64; Rev. 18:21).

Z. Babylon must be destroyed by God, not by man (Rev. 18:20) and it must be followed by the millennial reign of Christ (Rev. 19–20).

None of these scriptures have been fully fulfilled, so they must refer to the future destruction. Babylon was still a city in New Testament times, for Peter refers to a church at Babylon (1 Pet. 5:13) and the Babylonian Talmud of the Jews was produced there about 500 years after Christ. Since then Babylon has more or less been deserted and has gone into decay, but it has never been destroyed suddenly by God, as has been prophesied.

Revelation 18 definitely proves the existence of a literal city which will be destroyed under the seventh vial at the same time many other cities are destroyed. In Rev. 18:1-3 we have the indictment of Literal Babylon. In Rev. 18:4-8 we have God's verdict for her destruction. In Rev. 18:9-19 we have the lamentation over her destruction by the governmental, commercial, and maritime worlds. In Revelation 18:20 we have the rejoicing in Heaven over her destruction, and in Revelation 18:21-24 we have the cause and utter doom of Babylon predicted. The language is too simple and literal to make it mean anything but a description of the destruction of a literal city by an earthquake, as is plainly stated in Rev. 14:8; 16:17-21; 18:1-24; Isa. 13–14; Jer. 50–51.

Renovations could start in Shinar at any time and Babylon could be restored in a short while. In fact, work has already been done to restore the ruined walls of the city. At least seven years will transpire after the revelation of Antichrist to the destruction of Babylon under the seventh vial. All the above scriptures will be fulfilled in due time regardless of how impossible it seems to us of there being such a city in the last days. We conclude, therefore, that there are two Babylons in Rev. 1 and 18, Mystical Babylon and Literal Babylon.

Appendix One

BIBLICAL STUDIES

THE BIBLE IS EASY TO UNDERSTAND

We've reached the end of our study of Mystery Babylon, but we're not finished yet! God's Word presents us with a lifetime of study opportunities, but where are we supposed to start? This chapter is designed to give you the tools you'll need to study the Bible for yourself. The Bible is a simple book to understand. We've seen that as we've studied a topic that many consider complex and obscure. Even biblical prophecy, an area of Scripture that many assume to be beyond comprehension, is as easy to understand as the accounts of Jonah, Daniel or Joseph. This probably sounds ridiculous to most people, but perhaps considering a few simple facts will change your mind! Consider the following points:

The Bible is a Revelation. The Bible is an inspired revelation from God. A revelation is an uncovering or unveiling so that everyone may see what was previously covered or hidden.

The Bible Contains Many Repeated Truths. Over and over the Bible repeats truth so that "in the mouth of two or three witnesses every word may be established" (Dt. 17:6-7; 19:15; Mt. 18:16; 2 Cor. 13:1; 1 Tim. 5:19; Heb. 10:28). Because of this fact, any doctrine that is not plainly stated in Scripture is best left alone. When God says

> *All we need to do is to find out where "it is written" and then believe it. We must always make our ideas conform to the Bible and not the Scripture to our ideas.*

something about a particular topic, it will be found repeated in several places, so we will not be left in doubt as to what God says. Our part is to collect everything God says on a subject—making it so clear that no interpretation is necessary. If we do this, nothing will need to be added to or taken from the Bible in order to understand the truth. All we need to do is to find out where "it is written" and then believe it. We must always make our ideas conform to the Bible and not the Scripture to our ideas.

The Bible is Written in Simple Language. It is intended to be read and understood without interpretation. All God considers necessary to understand the Bible is childlike faith. God made both man and His Word, and they fit together as a lock and key (Job 32:8; 38:3-6; Jn. 1:4-9). Even the ungodly can understand if they so desire (Rom. 1:16-20).

The Bible is a Simple Book to Understand Because Most of it is Either History or Simple Instructions About How to Live. About 25,007 verses of the Bible—about 80 percent of it—contain simple history, commands, warnings, promises, rebukes, and plain instructions by means of which men may understand the will of God. The remaining 20 percent (or 6,207 verses) are prophecy written in the same simple human language that is used to record history. Of these 6,207 prophetic verses, 3,299 have been fulfilled and are now history. The 2,908 other verses are unfulfilled prophecy.

THE TRUE METHOD OF BIBLE INTERPRETATION

The fundamental principle is to gather from the Scriptures themselves the precise meaning the writers intended to convey. It applies to the Bible the same principles, rules, grammatical process, and exercise of common sense and reason that we apply to other books. In doing this, one must take the Bible as literal when it is at all possible. When a statement is found that cannot possibly be literal, as Jesus being a "door" or of a woman being clothed with the sun and standing on the moon and on her head a crown of twelve stars, or of land animals coming out of the sea, and other statements which are obviously not literal, then we know the language is figurative. In such cases we must get the literal truth conveyed by the figurative language, and the truth intended to be conveyed will be as literal as if it were expressed in literal language without the use of such figures. After all, figurative language expresses literal truth as much as if such figures were not used. In a general sense, the true method of Bible interpretation embraces the following ideas:

1. The primary meaning of words and their common use in the age in which they were used, and the importance of synonyms.
2. The grammatical construction and idiomatic peculiarities of the languages of the Bible, and the meaning of the context, both immediate and remote.
3. Comparison of parallel passages on the same subject.
4. The purpose or object of each writer in each particular book.
5. The historical background of each writer and the circumstances under which he wrote.
6. The general plan of the entire Bible, and its moral and spiritual teachings.
7. The agreement of Scripture in its several parts, and its prophecies and their fulfillment.

8. The manners and customs of the particular age and land of each writer.
9. Understanding of how to interpret prophecy, poetry, allegories, symbols, parables, figures of speech, types and all other forms of human expression.

When all these facts are kept in mind and all scriptures interpreted in harmony with all these principles, there cannot possibly be any misunderstanding of any part of the Bible.

GENERAL RULES OF BIBLE INTERPRETATION

1. The entire Bible came from God and possesses unity of design and teaching. We shall, therefore, consider both Testaments together as being equally inspired.

2. It may be assumed that no one resorts to speech or writing without having some idea to express; that in order to express that idea he will use words and forms of speech familiar to his hearers or readers; and that if he uses a word or figure of speech in a differ-

ent sense from what is commonly understood he will make the fact known.

3.   The Bible cannot contradict itself. Its teachings in one part must agree with its teachings in another part. Therefore, any interpretation which makes the Bible inconsistent with itself must rest upon false principles.

4.   No meaning should be gotten from the Bible except that which a fair and honest, grammatical, and historical interpretation yields.

5.   Language is an accumulation of words used to interchange thoughts. To understand the language of the speaker or writer, it is necessary to know the meaning of his words. A true meaning of the words is a true meaning of the sense. It is as true of the Bible as of any other book.

6.   Often to fully understand a passage of Scripture, the scope or plan of the entire book must be known. Sometimes the design of the books are made clear, as in the case

of Proverbs (1:1-4); Isaiah (1:1-3); John (20: 31); Revelation (1:1); etc. If the definite purpose of the book is not stated, the purpose of the book must be gotten from the contents and from the design of the Bible as a whole, as is clear in Jn. 5:39; 2 Tim. 2:15; 3:16-17. Some seeming contradictions are cleared up when this rule is observed. The difference between Paul and James is easily understood when the design of their books is understood and recognized. In Romans, Paul seeks to prove that a man is not saved by works, while in James he seeks to show that a man cannot remain saved unless he brings forth good works.

7. Sometimes the connection is obscured through the use of virtual dialogue between the writers and unseen persons, as in Ps. 15; Isa. 52:13; 63:1-6; Rom. 3; etc.

8. One of the most fundamental rules of interpretation is that of comparing Scripture with Scripture. It is by a strict and honest observance of this rule that the true meaning can be gotten when every other thing

has failed to make clear the meaning. Before arriving at the whole truth, be sure that all the scriptures on a subject are collected together and read at one time. If there is any question left after you have done this, then go over the whole subject carefully until every question is cleared up.

10.   In some places a statement on a subject may be very brief and seemingly obscure and will be made perfectly clear by a larger passage on the same subject. Always explain the seemingly difficult with the more simple scriptures. No doctrine founded upon a single verse of Scripture contains the whole of the subject; so do not be dishonest and wrest with Scripture or force a meaning into a passage that is not clearly understood in the passage or in parallel passages on the same subject.

11.   The progressive character of revelation and the gradual development of truth should be recognized. Some truths found in germ in the Old Testament are fully developed in the New Testament. For example, the idea of blood sacrifices was developed from

the time of Abel until it was fully culminated and made eternally clear in the sacrifice of Christ on Calvary.

12. The meaning of a word or phrase in the New Testament must not be carried back into Old Testament doctrine unless such is warranted by both Testaments. For example, water baptism, the Lord's Supper, and other New Testament doctrines are not found in the Old Testament at all. It is not proper to ask whether David was baptized in water, or whether Saul was a Christian, because these are New Testament terms.

13. Passages obviously literal should not be spiritualized. For example, making the natural blessings of Canaan the spiritual blessings of Heaven; regarding the ark of Noah as salvation through Christ, and hundreds of like interpretations.

14. The dispensational character of Scripture should be noted so that one can pigeon-hole every passage of Scripture in some definite period in God's plan.

15. The three classes of people (the Jews, the Church, and the Gentiles) dealt with in Scripture should be noted. Up to Genesis 12, the race as a whole is dealt with. From Gen. 12 to the New Testament the Jews and the Gentiles are dealt with; and in the New Testament these and the Church of God, made up of Jews and Gentiles, are dealt with (1 Cor. 10:32).

16. In all study of doctrine the practical aspect must be kept in view (2 Tim. 3:16-17).

17. The comparative importance of truth should be emphasized. The positive truths should be studied more than the negative. It is more important to have faith instead of unbelief; to know God better than Satan, etc. So one should learn more about faith and God than unbelief and Satan.

18. General familiarity with the Bible as a whole is very important. Keep reading the Bible over and over until its contents as a whole are familiar. The more one can remember here and there what he has read, the clearer the Bible will become.

19.   Words of Scripture must agree with the content and the subject matter in the passages where found. No meaning should be given to a word that would be in the least out of harmony with any Scripture. For example, the word "seen" in John 1:18 should be understood to mean "comprehended" in order to harmonize with all scriptures that state men saw God with the natural eyes.

20.   Careful attention should be paid to connecting words that connect events with each other, as the words "when," "then," etc., in Mt. 24:15-16, 21, 23, 40; 25:1.

21.   Careful attention should be paid to prepositions, definite articles, names of different persons and places with the same name, same persons and places with different names, and the names of different persons and places that are spelled differently by different authors in different books.

22.   Ascertain the exact meaning of the words of Scripture. The way a word is used, the subject matter, and the context often determine the true meaning.

23. Hebrew and Greek idioms should be noted. Sometimes a person having a peculiar characteristic, or subject to a peculiar evil, or destined to a particular destiny is called the child of that evil or destiny (Lk. 10:6; Eph. 2:1-3; 2 Thess. 2:3). The word "father" is applied to the originator of any custom or to the inventor of something (Gen. 4:20-21; Jn. 8:44). It is also used for "ancestor" (1 Chr. 1:17). The words "son" and "daughter" are sometimes used of descendants or in–laws. (Gen. 46:22; Lk. 3:23). The words "brother" and "cousin" are sometimes used of relatives and countrymen (Gen. 14:16 with 11:31; Lk. 1:36, 58). Names of parents are used of posterity (1 Ki. 18:17-18).

24. Preference is sometimes expressed by the word "hate" (Lk. 14:26; Rom. 9:13).

25. A peculiar idiom concerning numbers must be understood. Sometimes round numbers rather than the exact number are used (Jdg. 20:35, 46). This will explain seeming contradictions between numbers. Failure to understand this idiom may have caused

copyists and translators to misunderstand the numbers of some passages which seem erroneous and very large. For example, in 1 Sam. 6:19, we read the Lord smote in a very small town 50,070 people, which, in the Hebrew text reads, "seventy men two fifties and one thousand" or 70-100-1,000, or 1,170 people.

26. Careful attention should be paid to parenthesis, the use of italics (meaning these words are not in the original but supplied in English to make sense), the use of capital letters, marginal notes, references, summaries of chapters, chapter and page headings, the division of the text into chapters and verses, punctuation, obsolete English words, the rendering of the same original words by different English words, and other things about the English translations. All these things are human additions to the original text and should not be relied upon. For example, the running of references to prove a doctrine is sometimes misleading. The references may not be on the same subject, as can be easily detected by the reader.

27. Seeming contradictions in Scripture should be considered in the light of all the principles stated above. It must be kept in mind that the Bible records sayings of men under pressure of trials who said things that they never would have said otherwise. It records sayings of backsliders and rebels against God. It records statements of Satan and demons, and the words of such rebels should never be taken as the words from the mouth of God. They should not always be held as truth, for sometimes they are lies. Inspiration guarantees that these rebels said those things, but it does not guarantee that what they said is truth. Sometimes such statements contradict those of God and good men under divine utterance. Enemies of God take such contradictions between what God says and what rebels against God say and use them to prove the Bible contradicts itself. Naturally, such contradictions are found in the Bible, but they are not contradictions between statements made by God. The only statements that can be relied upon as truth are those that come from God and men who

speak for God as the Spirit gives utterance, and in these there is no contradiction.

The Bible also records the changes of God's will and plan in a later age over that of an earlier one. Such changes have been taken by the ungodly as contradictions, but such have had to be made by God because of the sin and rebellion of the people to whom He promised such things and for whom He made a certain plan. For example, in Gen. 1:31 God saw everything that He had made and it was good, but in Gen. 6:6 God repented that He had made man. In the meantime, between the two passages, sin and rebellion had entered, which made it necessary for God to have a changed attitude toward man. God has had to change his plan temporarily because of man's sin, but the original and eternal plan of God for creation has never been changed and never will be. God will finally realize His original purpose; that is the reason for His present dispensational dealings. God deals with each generation as circumstances demand. Sometimes God has had to change His promises to a certain group because they refused to meet the conditions for the fulfillment of these promises.

28. The seeming contradictions in the New Testament will also vanish and will be cleared up if men would be as fair with God as they will want God to be with them in the judgment. Always look for an explanation and it will be found. For example, men criticize the Bible for lack of harmony between the temptations of Christ in Mt. 4, and those in Lk. 4. But when we consider the fact that there were two separate sets of temptations during the forty days, and that after the first set of tests in Luke, Satan was dismissed "for a season," and after the last set of tests in Matthew, Satan was dismissed for good, there is no contradiction. The seeming contradictions between the sermons of Mt. 5 and Lk. 6 are cleared up when we see that there were two sermons—one on the mount and the other "in the plain." The so-called contradictions of the Bible are unreal and imaginary. Because of the lack of information as to the time, places, circumstances, etc., men cannot always judge concerning them. So it

would be best always to give God the benefit of the doubt, since He knows all things and was there when things happened. If He did not see fit to give all details so as to make every small detail clear, that is His wisdom. It should not detract from faith in God and His revelation.

All seeming contradictions in the Bible are easily cleared up with a better knowledge of the text, by correct translation, by knowing the manners and customs of the age and the country in which the books were written, by a wider application of historical facts, and by a fair and sane application of the rules of interpretation given above.

KEYS TO UNDERSTANDING THE BOOK OF REVELATION

I. Literalness of the Book

The book of Revelation admittedly contains both literal and figurative language. It is to be understood literally wherever possible. In other words, when a statement is made, it should be taken to mean just what is written unless such interpretation should be highly improbable and contrary to the dictates of rhetoric and spiritually-enlightened reason, or contrary to scriptures elsewhere on the same subject. In view of this test, if the passage does not admit a literal interpretation, then, of course, we must look elsewhere for an explanation. This is the only sound method of interpretation, as is clear from the fact that the book is a Revelation in itself. To treat it as a mystery or to spiritualize it is to deny what it professes to be. Every scene and every truth in the book is clearly explained in the book itself. The reader should first discover what the book itself says concerning its own truths and revelations before searching the remainder of the scriptures for additional light upon the subject in question. Pre-Revelation prophecy will throw much light upon many passages in Revelation and help in a more detailed study of almost every truth in the book. This Revelation is in perfect harmony with all the preceding prophecies and is the logical and harmonious completion of them.

II. The Key to the interpretation

> Write the things which thou hast seen, and the things which are, and the things which shall be hereafter (Rev. 1:19)

There is a natural three-fold division to the book of Revelation, as expressed in the verse cited above. One has only to believe this division, as given by Christ, to understand the book fully, especially as to the time of the fulfillment of the things of each division.

PART I. "The things which thou hast seen"; that is, Christ in the midst of the seven candlesticks (Rev. 1:12-18, 20), as seen by John before he began to write.

PART II. "The things which are"; that is, the things concerning the churches then existent and those which should exist throughout the church age to the rapture. This division takes in only Rev. 2–3.

PART III. "The things which shall be hereafter"; that is, the things which shall come to pass after the rapture of the Church. This division includes all of the events of Revelation 4–22.

The moment these divisions are forgotten and the reader begins to disarrange them and insert certain things into the one or the other that are not part of the division, he will become confused as to the divine order of these "things" which are so clearly given in consecutive order, and he will miss the true intent of the "things" written therein. That we refrain from confusing these "things" is absolutely imperative if a true understanding of them is to be gained.

To further prove that everything in Rev. 4-22 must occur after the rapture of the Church, we have this fact confirmed in Rev. 4:1. After John had recorded the vision of Christ in Rev. 1, completing the first division of the book, and after he had recorded all that Christ told him to write to the churches in Rev. 2-3, completing the second division of the book, he was told in Rev. 4:1 that he was to see "things which *must be* hereafter;" that is, after the things of the churches of the second division of the book. Therefore, if everything from Rev. 4:1 on through the rest of the book *must be* after the churches, then all the events of Rev. 4-22 must be after the churches. If they *must be* after the churches, then they cannot happen during the time of the churches. If they cannot happen during the time of the churches, then the Church is no longer on the earth during the fulfillment of the things which *must be* after the churches.

Revelation 4:1 literally reads in the Greek, "*After these things* [the things concerning the churches of the previous division] I saw, and behold a door opened in heaven, and the first voice [of Rev. 1:10] which I heard was as a trumpet speaking with me, saying, Come up hither, and I will show to thee *what things must take place after these things*;" that is, after the churches which he wrote about in the previous chapters.

These three divisions of Revelation mentioned above do not overlap, nor are they concurrent. One division must be completely fulfilled before the other begins. So if one will be fair and understand that every event of Rev. 4:1 on through the rest of the book *must be* fulfilled after the rapture of the Church, and if he does not bring one of these events back and place it among the churches as being fulfilled before the rapture, everything in the book will be clearly understood. Most of the false theories of Revelation have come into being because interpreters have failed to recognize the natural threefold division of the book. It is true, most interpreters emphasize these divisions in the beginning of their interpretations of the book, but when it comes to keeping all the events of Rev. 4–22 after the churches they generally fail to maintain their consistency. They will place some of the events of the seals, trumpets, and vials back in the church age and explain them as being fulfilled before the rapture. They will explain the woman and the manchild in con-

> *Most of the false theories of Revelation have come into being because interpreters have failed to recognize the natural threefold division of the book.*

nection with the Church of this age; whereas Jesus told John they were part of the "things" which *must be* after the churches. They will interpret the Dragon, the Beast, the False Prophet, or some other person or event of Revelation 4–22 as being fulfilled along with the churches, while the truth is they are part of the things which *must be* after the churches. If the reader will watch this he will at least be sensible enough to place these events of Revelation 4–22 where they belong—*after the churches*—and therefore, after the rapture of the Church.

III. The Division of the Book by Classes

1. Revelation 1–3 deals primarily with the church on earth.
2. Revelation 4–5 pictures the Church and the Old Testament saints with God in Heaven after the rapture, represented by the twenty-four elders.
3. Revelation 6–19 deals primarily with Israel under the last oppression by the Gentiles in fulfillment of Daniel's Seventieth Week after the rapture of the Church.
4. Revelation 20–22 refers to all three classes, the Church, the Jews, and the Gentiles. The earthly Jews will be the head of all earthly Gentiles and Christ with the Church will reign over both forever and ever.

IV. The Consecutive Order of Revelation

The book is a succession of consecutive events from the beginning to the end and is not unsystematic or confused. The events are to be taken in the order God gave them and not according to our own finite ideas as to their occurrence. However, it is almost universally recognized that Rev.1-5 and Rev.19-22 form a consecutive story. Therefore, we may logically conclude that the events of Rev. 6-18 are also consecutive in order. If the events of Revelation are not to be taken consecutively, upon what grounds do we attempt to fix another standard of arrangement? Where can we

> *The events are to be taken in the order God gave them and not according to our own finite ideas as to their occurrence.*

obtain any other authorized and authentic standard than that which is so plainly evident in the book itself? Why should we hopelessly confuse a plain prophecy given by the Lord concerning "things which must shortly come to pass" and change the order of events from that which was given by the Lord? Certainly He must have set forth the events in their proper order of fulfillment so that He would not confuse His servants.

V. The Outline of the Book of Revelation

INTRODUCTORY REMARKS
   (Rev. 1:1-11, 19).
   1. The Introduction (Rev. 1:1-3).
   2. The Salutation—From God the Father, Jesus Christ, and the Holy Spirit (Rev. 1:4-5a).
   3. The Exaltation—"Unto him that loved us . . . washed us . . . made us kings" (Rev. 1:5b-6).
   4. The Chief Theme of Revelation— "Behold he cometh with clouds" (Rev. 1:7).
   5. The Eternity of the Son of God— "I am Alpha and Omega" (Rev. 1:8).
   6. The Prophet—John and his commission to write (Rev. 1:9-11, 19).
   7. The Key to the Interpretation (Rev. 1:19).
I. "THE THINGS WHICH THOU HAST SEEN" (Rev. 1:12-18, 20).
   1. The Vision of Christ (Rev. 1:12-18).
   2. The Symbols of the Vision Interpreted (Rev. 1:20).
II. "THE THINGS WHICH ARE" (Rev. 2:1–3:22).

1. The things concerning the local church at Ephesus (Rev. 2:1-7).
2. The things concerning the local church at Smyrna (Rev. 2:8-11).
3. The things concerning the local church at Pergamos (Rev. 2:12-17).
4. The things concerning the local church at Thyatira (Rev. 2:18-29).
5. The things concerning the local church at Sardis (Rev. 3:1-6).
6. The things concerning the local church at Philadelphia (Rev. 3:7-13).
7. The things concerning the local church at Laodicea (Rev. 3:14-22).

III. "THE THINGS WHICH SHALL BE HEREAFTER" (Rev. 4:1–22:5).

1. The Heavenly Tabernacle—the raptured saints with God (Rev. 4:1–5:14).
   (1) The Heavenly Door (Rev. 4:1).
   (2) The Heavenly Throne (Rev. 4:2-3, 5).
   (3) The Heavenly Elders (Rev. 4:4).
   (4) The Heavenly Sea of Glass (Rev. 4:6b-8).
   (5) The Heavenly Living Creatures (Rev. 4:6b-8).

(6) The Heavenly Worship because of Creation (Rev. 4:9-11).

(7) The Heavenly Book (Rev. 5:1-4).

(8) The Heavenly Lamb (Rev. 5:5-7).

(9) The Heavenly Worship because of Worthiness to the Lamb (Rev. 5:8-14).

2. Daniel's Seventieth Week (Rev. 6:1–19:21; Dan. 9:27).

(1) The First Six Seals (Rev. 6:1-17).

(Parenthetical, Rev. 7:1-17).

(2) The Seventh Seal and First Six Trumpets (Rev. 8:1–9:21).

(Parenthetical, Rev. 8:2-6, 13; Rev. 10:1–11:13).

(3) The Seventh Trumpet (Rev. 11:14–13:18).

(Parenthetical, Rev. 14:1-20).

(4) The First Six Vials (Rev. 15:1–16:12).

(Parenthetical, Rev. 15:2-4; Rev. 16:13-16).

(5) The Seventh Vial (Rev. 16:17–18:24).

1. The Confirmation of Revelation (Rev. 22:6-7).
2. The Mistake in the Object of Worship (Rev. 22:8-9).
3. The Last Instructions (Rev. 22:10-19).
4. The Last Promise and Last Prayer (Rev. 22:20-21).

NOTES